*To Angie, Alia, and David, who shared my joy*
*in watching leopards in the Masai Mara.*

*Text and photographs copyright © 1991 by Jonathan Scott*
*First published in Switzerland under the title DAS LEOPARD-KINDER-BUCH*

*First published in the United States by Picture Book Studio Ltd.*
*Reissued in paperback in 1999 by North-South Books, an imprint of*
*Nord-Süd Verlag AG, Gossau Zürich, Switzerland.*

*Library of Congress Cataloging-in-Publication Data*
*Scott, Jonathan.*
*The leopard family book / by Jonathan Scott with photographs by the author.*
*Summary: Examines the family life, hunting patterns, territorial relationships,*
*and other activities that enable the leopard to survive in the wild.*
*1. Leopard—Juvenile literature. [1. Leopard.] I. Title*
*QL737.C23S35 1991*
*599.74′428—dc20 91-14578*

*A CIP catalogue record for this book is available from The British Library.*

*ISBN 0-7358-1212-8*
*10 9 8 7 6 5 4 3 2 1*
*Printed in Italy*

*Ask your bookseller for these other North-South Animal Family Books:*
*THE BEAVER FAMILY BOOK by Sybille and Klaus Kalas*
*THE CHIMPANZEE FAMILY BOOK by Jane Goodall*
*THE CROCODILE FAMILY BOOK by Mark Deeble and Victoria Stone*
*THE DESERT FOX FAMILY BOOK by Hans Gerold Laukel*
*THE ELEPHANT FAMILY BOOK by Oria Douglas-Hamilton*
*THE GRIZZLY BEAR FAMILY BOOK by Michio Hoshino*
*THE LION FAMILY BOOK by Angelika Hofer and Gunter Ziesler*
*THE PENGUIN FAMILY BOOK by Lauritz Somme and Sybille Kalas*
*THE POLAR BEAR FAMILY BOOK by Sybille Kalas and Thor Larsen*
*THE WHALE FAMILY BOOK by Cynthia D'Vincent*
*THE WILD HORSE FAMILY BOOK by Sybille Kalas*

*For more information about our books, and the authors and artists who create them,*
*visit our web site: http://www.northsouth.com*

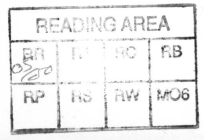

018

Jonathan Scott

# The Leopard
# Family Book

A MICHAEL NEUGEBAUER BOOK
NORTH-SOUTH BOOKS / NEW YORK / LONDON

It was the moment I had been waiting for all day. A pair of bright yellow eyes edged with green peered at me from over the top of the rocky ledge. It was a leopard, the most secretive and elusive of all the big cats.

I have been watching leopards in Africa for 15 years, yet I still feel as if I hardly know them. There is a great mystery hidden within those beautiful eyes.

As a young boy living on a farm in England, I often dreamed of visiting Africa to see the wild animals. My favorite outing was a visit to the London Zoo. I spent hours waiting in front of the enclosure where the leopard lived, hoping that it would emerge from its darkened den before I had to return home. That leopard taught me patience, and helped me learn that wild animals have a different sense of time than people do.

My dream of living among Africa's wild animals came true.

For the past 15 years I have lived in the Masai Mara National Reserve in Kenya, East Africa. The Mara is one of the finest wildlife areas in the world.

It is famous for its predators, the animals that hunt and eat other animals to survive. There are lions and hyenas, cheetahs and wild dogs, jackals and serval cats.

And leopards.

Leopards are the most adaptable and widely distributed of the large predators. They are found in the steamy jungles of Indonesia, the forests of India, and the rugged hills of Turkey and Israel. In Africa, leopards can still be found in the most impenetrable forests, at the edges of the open plains, on islands in lakes and rivers, and among the desert sands of the Kalahari.

Each leopard has a different pattern of spots and rosettes on its face and body, just like each person has a different set of fingerprints. By keeping a book of photographs of every leopard that I have seen, I can identify them as individuals. This identification is important to me, because for scientific study, it helps to be able to trace the experience and habits of particular animals.

This is the story of a very special leopard that I began observing when she was a small cub. I named her Chui, pronounced "chewy," which means "leopard" in Swahili, the national language of Kenya.

Imagine for a moment a domestic cat, the kind you would see curled up by the fireplace in someone's home. There is a lot about this house cat that is similar to Chui. They both have long curved tails that help them to keep their balance when they jump or climb trees. They both have long whiskers that they use to feel their way through tunnels in the long grass or bushes when they are hunting at night. And all cats possess sharp, curved claws on the front and back feet, which enable them to climb trees and to catch and hold their prey.

Of course, Chui is much bigger than any house cat. Leopards, lions, jaguars, tigers, snow leopards, clouded leopard, and cheetahs are known as the "big cats." All big cats, except cheetahs, can roar, but cannot purr. A house cat can purr, but cannot roar.

The leopard is not the largest of the big cats. In fact, most males weigh between 45 and 58.5 kilograms (100 and 130 pounds), which is less than one third the weight of an adult male lion or tiger. Male and female leopards look very similar to one another, except that males, like the one shown here, are considerably larger.

Leopards hunt mainly by sight and mostly at night. Their eyes are especially well adapted to allow them to hunt in the dark. They have wonderful hearing and can twist their ears to pick up the sound of their prey even when they cannot see it. Rubbery pads on the bottoms of their feet cushion each step and also enable them to walk silently as they hunt.

Leopards try to creep as close to their prey as possible and then, using strong back legs, they pounce or leap onto it. Powerful chest and front leg muscles give them tremendous strength to knock their prey down. Then with sharp claws they grab the animals they catch and keep them from getting away, biting into the throat to cut off the air supply.

The fur of some leopards is as pale as yellow grass, while others are the dark golden hue of an African sunrise. Each is patterned with spots and rosettes. The dappled colors of Chui's beautiful coat merge perfectly with the sunlight and shadows, helping to conceal her from her prey and hide her from her enemies. I have seen Chui stand so still and blend so perfectly that unless she were to move, you would never see her.

Chui can run with the speed of a sprinter, and leap and pounce with the agility of a gymnast. She can do things that no lion or cheetah would dream of attempting. For instance, she can claw her way up the vertical trunk of a tree with 25 kilograms of meat clamped in her jaws – that's almost 60 pounds of dead weight. Or she can snatch a bird from the air with an outstretched paw. These are the kind of extraordinary abilities that make the leopard my favorite animal.

Leopards are creatures of the night. To try to find Chui, I had to search for her while she was still moving about during the cooler hours of the early morning.

There were many days when I could find no trace of her. Yet I knew she was somewhere close, crouched behind a rocky ledge, or perhaps sitting motionless behind a curtain of head-high grass, or sprawled lazily in a giant fig tree, watching as I drove past in my safari vehicle. Occasionally I was lucky and Chui might make a movement just as I cast my eyes in her direction. What a joy it was whenever I found her.

Chui roamed an area of fifteen square kilometers, which is about six square miles. This "home range" is where she finds food and water, where she can hide from lions and hyenas, and where she can find a mate and raise her cubs. Adult leopards tend to avoid contact with one another, although females will sometimes share part of the same home range.

Like all leopards, Chui marks her home range in several ways. Using urine tinged with the pungent odor of anal glands, she sprays a powerful scent onto bushes and trees.

She also scratches the bark of trees with her claws, and at various times during the night, calls quite loudly. With these messages, she communicates with other leopards without having to come face-to-face with them and risk being injured in a battle. While leopards generally avoid fighting, a male will occasionally fight to defend the females living in his territory.

Among all the members of the cat family, only the lions are truly social animals, which means that they live together in groups. A group of lions is called a pride, and it is made up of several females and two or three adult males. Leopards are more typical as cats, for they are solitary. Except for mating times and when she has cubs to care for, Chui lives alone.

For all cats facial expressions are a very important means of communication. The expression of the eyes, the position of the ears, the attitude of the lips and teeth, everything has a meaning. These visual signals, along with sounds – growling, snarling, coughing, spitting, and hissing – convey powerful messages of aggression and submission.

These cubs were not born in Leopard Gorge, but at another of Chui's favorite resting places – an enormous cave along Fig Tree Ridge. Chui would have preferred the safety and familiarity of Leopard Gorge, but she found that a lioness had recently given birth to cubs there, so she had to go to the nearby cave. Here she gave birth to two cubs, both males.

I did not see much of Chui's cubs during the first few weeks of their lives, for they remained concealed in the darkened cave. Chui spent a lot of time with her cubs during these early days so they could suckle from her milk-laden teats. When she wanted to move the cubs she carried them by the scruff of their necks just like a domestic cat would do.

By the time the cubs were about four weeks old, they had already tasted meat. Sometimes Chui came back to her cubs with a warthog piglet or an impala fawn clasped in her mouth. She would drop the kill at their feet so they could gorge themselves. Then she would feed herself.

Even when they were just two months old, I could distinguish between the cubs. One was a bossy little fellow who always insisted on suckling from the two teats closest to his mother's head. Each cub knew his correct position, which helped to prevent them from squabbling – and from clawing and scratching their mother. The cubs continued to suckle throughout the first six months of their lives.

Since male leopards play no part in rearing cubs, the female must nurture them by herself. Chui was fiercely protective of her cubs, and threatened any intruder by hissing and growling. This would slow down an enemy's approach, giving her cubs the chance to seek shelter. Lions, hyenas, male leopards, and even baboons, jackals, and large eagles are capable of killing leopard cubs. This is why it is a considerable triumph for a mother leopard to raise even one of the cubs from her litter.

Chui used a variety of calls to communicate with her cubs. One unusual sound she frequently used was a series of short, sharp sounds, like someone puffing or sniffing. These sounds are called prusten.

The cubs recognized this sound and would rush from the cave to greet their mother. Chui also used a variety of "auu" and "iauu" sounds for the same purpose. If they strayed or if she needed the cubs to follow her, Chui would use her special calls. And if the cubs became lost or distressed, they used their own high-pitched "iauu" to call for help.

Chui was particularly wary of the many lions that shared her home range. She knew that they would try to kill her cubs if they found them. The cave and the rocky area surrounding it provided good cover for her and her little family, but as the cubs became more active, Chui was constantly alert for danger.

There were other dangers that kept Chui busy as well. The cave that Chui had chosen as the hiding place for her cubs was situated within 100 meters (over 100 yards) of two giant fig trees, a favorite roosting place for a troop of more than 80 olive baboons. Far from avoiding contact with the leopards, the troop, led by big male baboons, tended to mob and terrorize Chui and her cubs. They wanted to be sure Chui would choose to hunt elsewhere.

During the daytime when the baboons were active, Chui kept her cubs close by, and maintained a watchful eye on her noisy neighbors.

Spotted hyenas are the most common large predator of the Mara Reserve, and show little respect for anything smaller than a lion.

When Chui hunted, even a single hyena was usually able to rob her of her kill, unless she reached the safety of a tree before one arrived. Hyenas have feet like dogs, they do not have the sharp retractable claws that enable cats to climb trees. Because Chui hunted alone, when threatened by hyenas she would usually abandon her kill rather than risk injury. But occasionally, she would resist these attempts to steal her hard-earned food, and lash out with impressive ferocity.

Chui hunted according to the changing seasons. Mainly she killed impala and Thomson's gazelles, but when the warthog piglets and other young animals were abundant during the rainy season, she focused on these. Topi calves, young wildebeest and zebra foals, dìk dik, jackals, African hares, and hyrax all helped to provide Chui with ample food for her cubs.

The cubs were almost four months old when Chui led them for the first time to a kill she had safely stored in a tree. By now the cubs had perfected their climbing skills and could clamber up to the top of the tallest tree.

Leopard cubs do not like sharing food. They squabbled and growled, spat and clawed at each other while trying to manoeuvre for position around the carcass. Because it is the nature of leopards to be alone and fend for themselves, Chui's cubs were much more fierce with each other than lion or cheetah cubs of a similar age would have been. Chui was quick to intervene, biting down over their necks to force them apart. The cubs soon learned that it was easier to take turns feeding than to fight.

You may have noticed that a domestic cat has a rough tongue, and seen how a cat uses its tongue to groom itself. For a leopard, the tongue is more than just a convenient comb. A leopard's tongue is so rough because it is used for grooming but it can also be used to scrape the last scraps of meat from bones.

The leopards' high protein diet allows them to spend most of the time resting, sometimes as much as 20 hours a day. While they prefer to kill and eat antelope and other small animals, when food is scarce a leopard will eat anything—snakes, insects, fruit, even rotten meat.

The cubs were always delighted whenever Chui returned from hunting, greeting her by sinuously rubbing alongside her legs and body, pushing their heads up under her chin and against her face – much as a house cat does when it wants a bowl of milk.

As the cubs grew older, Chui spent more and more time on her own, patrolling the full extent of her home range in pursuit of food.
The two youngsters were extremely playful and amused themselves for hours. They flipped over rocks, chewed sticks, belly-flopped onto plants, and scrambled around in the bushes. Sometimes Chui abandoned her aloof, adult demeanor and joined the cubs in their games, leaping into the air, ambushing the cubs and then pouncing on them. This also helped to develop their hunting skills and to acquaint them with the rough and tumble of adulthood.

Watching these leopards had been the highlight of my years in Africa, and I wish it could have gone on forever. But one day Chui and her cubs simply vanished. I still would set out as usual before sunup each day, as I had for the past six months, but there was no sign of the leopards. I knew that by this time the cubs were old enough to follow their mother anywhere, so I searched far and wide, visiting the giant fig trees, the rocky outcrops, and all the other favorite resting places where I had seen them in the past. But Chui and her cubs were nowhere to be found.

Even today, many years after I last saw Chui and her cubs, whenever I see a leopard I always check the spot markings on its coat, hoping that it may be one of those big cats that I came to know so well.